AF335067

Original title:
A Palindrome of Eternal Knowing

Author: Hugo Fitzgerald
ISBN HARDBACK: 978-3-69080-215-4
ISBN PAPERBACK: 978-3-69080-710-4

Knowledge's Embrace

In a world where facts collide,
The guru's hat feels far too wide.
With wise cracks flying here and there,
I question if they're really rare.

Oh wisdom, please, where's your finesse?
I laughed so hard, I made a mess.
The books I read all tell me so,
But who's the fool? I just don't know.

Within the Echo Chamber

In rooms where laughter bounces back,
I think I've lost my mental track.
My thoughts are shared, but oh, beware!
The echo keeps much more to share.

Round and round, it's quite the ride,
Where sense and nonsense both reside.
A circle jerk of thoughts, so wild,
I'm both the sage and giggling child.

The Thread of Time

Time's a jester with no regard,
It plays with clocks, oh my, how hard!
I thought I'd grasp its fleeting flight,
But found my socks still out of sight.

It stretches thin, then pulls me back,
A tug-of-war on reason's track.
With every thought I try to catch,
It slips away—quite the mismatched.

Harmony in Repetition

Oh joy, it's time for fun again,
The same old joke, the same old pen.
Why write anew when old ones thrill?
I laugh again; it fits the bill.

In circles, I repeat the jest,
Each punchline lands just like the rest.
Yet every time my friends all cheer,
It seems no one can shed a tear!

The Looping Narrative

I woke up today, not a clue,
What day it was, the world's askew.
My coffee's cold, my socks don't match,
The cat's outside, a strange mustache.

I turned around, then spun again,
Is this the start or just the end?
The mirror laughed, it took my place,
I think I'll join, embrace this chase.

The sun came up to say hello,
But was it night? I just don't know.
My calendar's a wiggly worm,
It wriggles fast, a funky term.

In circles, I dance, round and round,
My thoughts like kites that can't be found.
So here I go, back to the start,
With giggles bright, and a funny heart.

Stars in Orbit

Stars twinkle bright, but why can't they sit?
They spin around, like they're having a fit.
A cosmic dance, with planets that swirl,
The galaxy jokes, in an endless twirl.

Saturn wears rings, it's quite a sight,
But why do they spin, day and night?
Jupiter winks, with a mischievous grin,
While comets race by, in a flashy spin.

The moon tells tales, of a night gone wild,
As if it's still dreaming, like a lost child.
Constellations chuckle, in patterns so free,
Galactic giggles, across the big sea.

In this vast space, it's a funny game,
With everyone laughing, no one to blame.
They loop and they swirl, in an endless run,
The stars in their orbits, having such fun!

The Cycle Continues

In a world that spins 'round, oh so quick,
We chase our own tails, a comical trick.
Round and round, we laugh at the chase,
Finding our socks in a strange, merry place.

Gravity holds us, like a playful friend,
We twirl in circles, there's no need to bend.
A cat on a leash turns in joyous delight,
As we dance through the day into a starry night.

Timeless Reverberations

Time ticks on, but where is the clock?
We giggle and frolic, we've lost our tick-tock.
Did we go forward, or swing back to the start?
With endless questions, oh, where's the smart part?

Echoes of laughter, a sound that persists,
Bouncing off walls in a myriad of twists.
Like a rubber ball, we just can't sit still,
In a game of charades, we're all at a thrill.

Labyrinth of Self

So many mirrors in this curious maze,
We nod at reflections, lost in a daze.
Hey, is that me? No, it's just my twin,
With a grin that says, let's just spin again!

We zig and we zag, with each choice we make,
Finding ourselves in each humorous mistake.
The exit's elusive, but laughter we share,
In the tangled strands of our whimsical hair.

Unraveling the Infinite

Loops and knots in the strings of our fate,
We fumble and stumble, but isn't it great?
Unwind the mystery, giggle with glee,
For every great puzzle is a chance to be free.

Like a spaghetti strand on a rollercoaster ride,
We loop-de-loop on the fun slide outside.
Discovering truths in a bubble of cheer,
As we unravel the infinite, all is made clear.

Reflections in Still Water

In the pond, frogs play tricks,
Ripples dance to fun-filled licks.
What's that sound? It's just the breeze,
Or maybe grandma, chasing bees!

Fish swim by in silly suits,
Taking selfies in their boots.
A turtle winks with a cheeky grin,
"Come join us, let the fun begin!"

Secrets of the Universe

Stars giggle in the night sky,
Caught in a game, oh my, oh my!
Aliens read our birthday cards,
"Humans make things pretty hard!"

Planets play leapfrog, it's true,
While comets sing the cosmic blues.
In this chaos, a laugh is found,
Too funny, just spinning round and round!

The Endless Inquiry

Why is that cat stuck on a roof?
Asks the dog, chasing his goof.
"Because it thinks it's a bird, oh dear!"
"Next question! Bring on the cheer!"

Balloons float on a whimsy quest,
"Is it a party? Or just a jest?"
Every answer leads to more,
As questions dance on a funny floor!

Roots of Knowing

Trees whisper secrets, roots intertwined,
"What do you know? I'm half-maligned!"
Squirrels chuckle through each branch,
"Tell us more! Let's take a chance!"

The wise old owl plays games of doubt,
"Did I hoot? Or was it a shout?"
With laughter echoing through the haze,
Life's mysteries dance in playful ways!

Whirls of Knowledge

Round and round the wisdom spins,
Ideas dance like little pins.
Up and down, we laugh, we cheer,
Curious minds with nothing to fear.

Witty minds in a playful race,
Chasing thoughts all over the place.
Giggles echo, insights sprout,
In this whirl, there's never a doubt.

Wisdom's trick, a silly jest,
Learning's game, we never rest.
Jokes and giggles fill the air,
Who knew knowledge could be so rare?

In this loop, we take a ride,
With each twist, our hearts collide.
Laughter rings, a joyful sound,
In this circle, truth is found.

The Timeless Quest

Through space and time, we wander free,
A treasure hunt for you and me.
Tick-tock goes the clock's parade,
As silly rhymes in whispers fade.

Seek and find, the jesters grin,
In riddles, we lose, but then we win.
Questions fly like birds in song,
The timeless quest keeps us strong.

Oh what fun, this search of lore,
Silly tales behind each door.
The answer's just a giggle away,
In this quest, we laugh and play.

Maps are silly, drawn with crayons,
Leading us to spots of mayhem.
But here we stand, hands in the air,
In the journey, joy we declare.

Paths Intertwined

In twisty lanes, our fates align,
Where laughter meets the grand design.
We trip and tumble through the night,
In every fall, a spark of light.

Paths are crossed with silly flair,
In each misstep, we find our share.
Witty banter fills the lane,
In this tangle, there's no pain.

Connections made with every turn,
In crooked paths, we brightly learn.
Twists and turns make life a treat,
In this dance, we find our beat.

When life's a maze, we draw a smile,
And walk together, mile by mile.
Paths entwined in joyful thread,
With every laugh, we forge ahead.

The Shimmer of Infinity

Stars twinkle in a cosmic jest,
In the vastness, we take our rest.
Life's a loop, a funny game,
Infinity's just another name.

Waves of thought crash on the shore,
Ideas bounce, we laugh and roar.
In the shimmer, we lose our way,
But in that glow, we choose to play.

Time's a prankster, oh so sly,
It stretches long, it loves to fly.
With every giggle, moments fold,
Infinity is bright and bold.

So grab a star, make a wish,
In the chaos, there's always bliss.
With each chuckle, life's a show,
In this shine, we dance and glow.

The Continuum of Thought

In the middle of my mind,
Thoughts spin round like a squirrel chined.
Ideas bounce off walls like a ball,
Yet never seem to answer the call.

Tick-tock, says the clock on the wall,
Whispering secrets that make me enthrall.
What is nonsense? What is wise?
I can't help but giggle at these lies!

Banana peels on the path I tread,
Wobbling thoughts dance in my head.
If I chase them too fast they won't obey,
They'll spiral back to laugh at my dismay!

So I sit in this surreal groove,
Life's a puzzle that won't quite move.
Each loop I take is an endless quest,
Finding the funny in this jest.

Unbroken Circles

Around and around, a joke goes 'round,
Like a lost puppy that can't be found.
One ear to the ground, the other in space,
Watch it spin, it's a dizzy race!

A cat in a hat sings a silly tune,
Under a bright and chuckling moon.
What is the punchline? Why so absurd?
Don't ask me! I'm lost in my own word.

Chasing my tail is a daily routine,
Seems like I'm stuck in a funny machine.
A loop-de-loop with a side of cheer,
Gravity giggles, "You're stuck right here!"

But I'll take a twirl and share a grin,
Life's just a circle that turns with a spin.
In unbroken circles, we'll laugh and play,
Finding the humor in every ray.

The Dance of Reflection

In the mirror, I see a twisty face,
Making funny poses in this crowded space.
Reflection giggles and pulls a prank,
I wonder if it knows how to thank!

Two left feet in a right-hand world,
My steps go flailing, my thoughts unfurled.
The dance of delight on a slippery floor,
Each misstep's an encore, never a bore!

A waltz with wisdom, I trip and fall,
Laughter echoes down the hallway hall.
Every stumble's a chance for a rhyme,
Bouncing back is the best of the clime!

So I'll dance with shadows, twirling around,
In this carnival of thoughts, I'm glory-bound.
With every reflection, I chuckle anew,
It's funny to think I'm just dancing with you!

Spheres of Insight

In a world of bubbles, thoughts collide,
Pop! goes logic, like a cork-topped ride.
Round and round, silly things float,
Sinking deep like a heavy old boat.

A sphere of wisdom, or is it a game?
Each question asked is more of the same.
What's upside down? What's right-side up?
Laughing with circles, I sip from my cup.

Rolling through ideas, I tumble and dive,
Finding the joke keeps my thoughts alive.
Wisdom giggles, "Come join in the fray!"
Life's just a ball, so let's laugh and play!

With every bounce, new tales emerge,
Each sphere of insight begins to surge.
A chorus of giggles in every round,
Finding the funny in knowledge profound!

Tapestry of Time

We weave our tales, so bold and bright,
Each loop spins laughter, a pure delight.
The past is present, isn't that keen?
A jester's hat in a time machine.

Socks with sandals, a fashion faux pas,
Yet here we stand, with joy, huzzah!
Each moment a stitch, in life's grand play,
Laughing at how we dance the day away.

The Wisdom We Wear

In polka dots, wisdom rides along,
A quirky punchline to life's silly song.
We wear our knowledge like a two-headed hat,
Forward and backward; imagine that!

With clown shoes tied for a serious meeting,
Our thoughts meander, oh how they're fleeting!
Beneath the laughter, nuggets of gold,
Silly secrets in stories retold.

Backward Glances

We trip on memories, tumbling back,
An old rubber chicken in our backpack.
Chasing our tails in a merry round,
Finding punchlines that never were found.

The echoes of giggles haunt our ears,
Like the whispering wind, it tickles our fears.
With each backward glance, a chuckle we share,
These moments of joy, beyond all compare.

The Unfolding Story

Once upon a sneeze, a story began,
With a frog wearing boots and a funky tan.
Each page flips backwards, oh what a sight,
A hero's large hat, too big for the fight.

With laughter we scribble, our plot thickens fast,
A tale full of whimsy, that's surely a blast.
We unwind the yarn, let humor unfold,
In a world where the silly is always bold.

Patterns in the Cosmos

Stars dance in the sky,
Planets wink as they twirl.
Comets sneeze, oh my!
Galaxies spin in a whirl.

Laughing nebulae beam,
While asteroids tell tales,
Space is but a dream,
In cosmic, wobbly trails.

Meteorites with quirks,
Chase moons doing chores.
Each orbit has its perks,
Galactic laughter roars.

Constellations giggle,
Mapping out the night.
Each twinkle, just a wiggle,
In this grand starry sight.

The Sphinx's Riddle

What walks on four paws?
Then two, then three it goes.
A riddle that gives pause,
With answers in a prose.

Sphinx sighs, dust in air,
Whispers secrets so sly.
Chasing tails, without care,
To solve, give it a try.

Cats know the deep lore,
They perch on the high shelf.
The answer, it's no bore,
Just take a look at yourself!

Laughing at the bliss,
Of riddles wrapped in jest.
The answer's a big kiss,
By life, we're all addressed.

Echoes of the Past

Whispers in the breeze,
History claps and cheers.
Old trunks hold memories,
Full of giggles and sneers.

Footsteps dance like ghosts,
In shoes too big to wear.
Echoes toast to their hosts,
With stories always there.

Pages flip with a grin,
As secrets swirl and sway.
What could've been, what's been,
Is just a game we play.

Time twirls in a play,
With laughter as its friend.
Each moment, come what may,
Is just a means to bend.

Each Step a Reflection

On paths where shadows prance,
We trip over our thoughts.
Every step, a new chance,
In silliness, we've caught.

Puddles mirror our fun,
We leap and splash around.
Life is just a pun,
In laughter, we are found.

Flip-flops sing a tune,
As we rush to be late.
Bouncing like a balloon,
With giggles as our fate.

Every twist and turn shows,
How silly we can be.
In life's wild, wacky flows,
We dance, so joyfully.

The Convergence of Paths

Two roads meet in silly dance,
And giggle at a whispered chance.
They twist and turn, then shout hooray,
For every wrong will find its way.

A spaghetti bowl of tangled lines,
Where lost socks laugh and play in shrines.
The signs are flipped, the map's a joke,
Discovery's laugh is all bespoke.

Be not alarmed when you get lost,
For every turn has its own cost.
The paths may stretch toward bizarre,
Yet every wanderer is a star.

And when the journey seems absurd,
Just flip it back, you've surely heard.
For every pathloops in a grin,
With every end, the start begins!

Reflections of Existence

Mirror, oh mirror, what do you see?
A jester who forgot his glee?
A face that grins, yet seems quite blue,
Winks at itself, then starts anew.

Existence quips, it's light as air,
A juggling act without a care.
Where thoughts collide, they crack a smile,
And life looks back with playful style.

Life's a joke told in a crowded room,
With punchlines tossed like flowers in bloom.
Yet every jest can twist and bend,
And teach us all that we depend.

So laugh, dear friend, at what we hold,
For wisdom's wrapped in tales retold.
As reflections twist, they dance and twine,
In this grand show, we intertwine.

Threads of the Unknown

An endless spool of yarn unfurls,
Spinning tales of boys and girls.
Each thread a path, a quirky dance,
Woven tales that twist by chance.

The unknown giggles, it takes its time,
With every knot, an awkward rhyme.
It pulls and tugs, a playful tease,
Unraveling riddles with the greatest ease.

Once tangled up, oh what a sight,
In chaos, we find the sheer delight.
For every twist, a story's there,
Laced in laughter, grounded in air.

So hold the threads, both soft and wild,
Embrace the dance, be silly, child.
In every weave, a jest is spun,
For in the unknown, we find our fun.

The Sway of Being

In a world that sways with a cheeky grin,
Life tiptoes in, ready to spin.
It dances lightly on a whim,
And sings a tune that's far from grim.

Being, oh being, what a funny mix,
Like juggling eggs with a bag of bricks.
It swirls about, a joyful fright,
In every stumble, a sense of light.

So sway along with all your might,
And waltz through days both bright and slight.
For every step in silly play,
Reveals the dance of every day.

When life gets crazy, make it bold,
And in the sway, find stories told.
For being's laughter never ends,
In quirks and twists, the heart transcends.

Layers of Truth

Peel back the layers, what do you find?
A potato or onion, both take their time.
Truth hides beneath skins, with humor it plays,
In the puzzle of life, we're all in a maze.

Round and round we go, like a wheel on a bike,
Chasing our tails, oh what a sight!
Answers are giggles, in the search for the wise,
In the layers of truth, there's always a surprise.

Resonance of Understanding

Bouncy like rubber, thoughts fly in the air,
Understanding wobbles, oh what a flair!
Echoes of laughter, in the hall of our minds,
Resonate softly, the truth that unwinds.

Jokes traded like currency, wisdom like gold,
In the game of perception, the new and the old.
Tickles and chuckles, the sound of the core,
Understanding dances, asking for more.

Echoing Horizons

Look to the horizon, what do you see?
A giant gopher, or just me on a spree?
Echoes of laughter, from mountains to seas,
A giggle or two, life's simple keys.

Horizons are funny, stretching too far,
Chasing a mirage, under the stars.
In the vastness we wander, with smiles we ignite,
Echoes of joy, in the dark of the night.

Tales of the Infinite

Gather 'round quietly, let's spin a yarn,
Of cats who drive taxis, and pigs on a farm.
Infinite tales, both silly and sweet,
In the land of the absurd, reality's beat.

Frogs who wear glasses, and cows who can't sing,
Infinite stories, oh what fun they bring!
In the laughter of ages, wisdom shines bright,
Tales of the infinite, a jubilant sight.

The Bridge of Wholeness

Across the bridge, I'll strut and sway,
A chicken dances, hip hooray!
With each odd step, I trip and fall,
A graceful swan, nobody's call.

In mirrored laughs, we share the glee,
A juggling cat, now that's my key!
With witty puns that never end,
I'll be the punchline, my dear friend.

Tides of Clarity

The waves come in, no boat in sight,
I surf on squirrels, oh what a fright!
With jelly beans to steer my way,
I'll navigate this gumdrop bay.

A fish in socks, I can't resist,
With bubbles bursting, add to the mist!
The tides bring laughs, not just the blue,
But jellybeans in a pirate's shoe.

The Rewind of Thought

Press rewind, what came before?
A chicken dressed in dinosaur!
I laughed so hard, I lost my snack,
The roll went wild, that sneaky pack.

Oh, twist my mind, like pretzel dough,
A binge on thoughts, they come and go.
The world's a movie, laughtrack loud,
With nonsensical scenes, I'm so proud!

Ever-Present Awareness

A thought appears, then takes a spin,
Like squirrels on skateboards, where to begin?
With radishes dancing, they steal the show,
My mind's a circus, who needs to know?

In moments flashing, time goes fast,
A wiggling worm, what a blast!
Awareness tickles, gleeful delight,
I trip on laughter, what a sight!

The Gathering of Moments

In a room full of clocks, they all tick in sync,
A chair that talks back, and we're on the brink.
Pancakes do flips, while the syrup takes flight,
Time's just a jester, with laughter in sight.

We danced with our shadows, in shoes two sizes too big,
A cat in a top hat, who just loves to dig.
With each twist and turn, we looped back to fun,
Like a rubber band snapping, it's just begun.

The jellybeans giggled, as they rolled down the hall,
Bananas were singing, while playing football.
A grand tea party hosted by mischievous mice,
In a place where the weirdness is often quite nice.

So gather your moments, in jars on the shelf,
And laugh with the chaos, it's good for your health.
For time's just a circle that loves a good prank,
Join the gathering joy, let's fill up the tank.

Through an Endless Lens

Peering through glasses that bend time and space,
A chicken in sneakers tries to win a race.
With every snapshot, the world gets a tweak,
A fish with a tutu flashes quite the chic.

We wandered through frames, every moment a scene,
Where ducks wore bow ties, and squirrels held a dream.
The lens laughs and winks, a playful charade,
As our giggles reflect in the memories made.

A pancake brigade marches with syrupy pride,
While clouds shape their stories, in the bright sky wide.
We surf on nostalgia, like waves at the shore,
Each laugh a snapshot, we just can't ignore.

So adjust the focus; let the silliness shine,
In this funhouse of moments, it's simply divine.
Through an endless lens, we capture what's true,
In the gallery of giggles, there's always room for you.

Twin Flames of Insight

Two candles burn bright, their flames dance around,
With thoughts that combine, in a whirl, they're unbound.
One's wearing a hat, while the other has shoes,
In this bizarre mix, we can't choose our views.

They whisper sweet secrets, like gossiping friends,
With jokes that unravel and laughter transcends.
Like two peas in a pod, they bounce to and fro,
Illuminating moments and tickling the glow.

In twin paradoxes they challenge our wit,
With riddles and giggles, they just never quit.
So light up your candles, let insights ignite,
In the glow of their wisdom, we find sheer delight.

As sparks fill the air, embrace what you see,
In the dance of the flames, we're all meant to be free.
Together we'll frolic, in sparks that entwine,
With twin flames of insight, we eternally shine.

Waves of Memory

The ocean of moments flows in, then retreats,
With surfboards of laughter, it's never discreet.
Each wave carries whispers of stories untold,
As jellyfish chuckle at memories bold.

The tides bring us riddles, wrapped up in a splash,
Where sea cucumbers play games in a dash.
We ride on the wave, like surfboards in flight,
With dolphins that giggle, it's pure delight.

They say time's a current, ever flowing away,
But in the sea of memory, we dive and we play.
Each bubble reflects a familiar old face,
In the waves of the joyous, we find our true place.

So let's dance on the shoreline, with laughter and cheer,
For waves of memory bring everyone near.
In oceans of humor, we make our own way,
With every new tide, there's more joy to display.

The Within that Holds Without

Within the brain, thoughts twirl around,
Like squirrels playing tag on the ground.
One says, "Jump!" while the other says, "Sit!"
In a riddle, they laugh, just a tad bit lit.

Outside the window, a cat chases a leaf,
It thinks it's a foe, the ultimate thief.
But oh, how it pounces, then stumbles in play,
A bounding ball of fluff, who thought it could slay?

Wisdom whispers silly things in our ear,
Like, "Why does the moon glow while the sun drinks
beer?"
We ponder and snicker, finding it odd,
Reality flips, like a comedic facade.

Deep in the always, laughter resides,
In the echoes of knowing, where joy never hides.
We dance and we wiggle, not wanting to quit,
For the fun lies within this curious skit.

Wisdom that Reflects Back

Wisdom wears glasses, peering askew,
It reads the fine print, and shrugs at the view.
"Did I just grow wiser, or is that just my hat?"
A deep breath of laughter flows, just like that.

Mirrored reflections show truths that we see,
A chicken in front, while it clucks with glee.
It asks, "What's the matter, did I cross the street?"
The answer is simple, it just likes to eat!

Flipping through moments, we trip and we fall,
Bananas peel wisdom, they giggle and call.
"Slip on my wisdom, it's perfectly fine,
For learning's a dance, like sipping on wine."

So gather the quirks, let laughter rings out,
For wisdom that reflects is what life's all about.
In the echo of giggles, we swirl round and round,
Discovering joy, where fun can be found.

Unfolding Realities Revisited

Once in a dream, an onion wore shoes,
It danced on the table, dodging some blues.
With layers of laughter, it twirled in delight,
Creating a ruckus that brightened the night.

In the land of the wobbling, the cups have a chat,
One dreams of a baby, the other a cat.
"Let's brew some tea with the cookies we made,
And gossip 'bout stars in the lemonade shade!"

Rabbits in bowties discuss their grand schemes,
While worms practice tap dance, fulfilling their dreams.
Each twist of existence unfolds with a grin,
For realities bend where the giggles begin.

So spin and unravel the fabric of time,
With tales that are silly and utterly prime.
In the playful embrace of the whimsical dance,
We find in our laughter, we take the chance.

The Mirror of Unseen Truths

A mirror reflects what we wish it to be,
A lion or puppy, it's all up to me.
"Who's the fairest?" the mirror does chuckle,
When a raccoon in pajamas stirs up some trouble.

Peeking through wisdom, we giggle in shock,
For the truth is a package wrapped tight with a lock.
"Does this make me look tall, or just two feet wide?"
The answer is simple; it's best when you glide.

Oh, the truths that run wild in the corners of chants,
Silliness blooms in the oddest of plants.
In gardens of laughter, where thoughts come alive,
We wear our reflections like clothes; let them thrive.

So let's raise a toast in this whimsical spree,
To the mirror of truths that can never quite see.
In the realm of the funny, we're free to explore,
For laughter is wisdom, and wisdom's the core.

The Loop of Awareness

In circles we go, round and round,
Chasing our tails, never quite found.
The cat calls us silly, what do we care?
We giggle and spin, with nary a glare.

Thoughts play a game of hide and seek,
Echoes of laughter, quirky and meek.
We ponder and joke, then tumble anew,
Awareness is fuzzy, like a well-worn shoe.

Each question we ask, the answer's unclear,
"Do fish play chess?"—now that's a fine cheer!
With a wink and a nod, we stay on this ride,
In loops of perception where quirks can't hide.

So let's spin our minds, let confusion flow,
In the loop of awareness, together we'll glow.
We'll laugh at the nonsense, the weirdness we find,
In this brilliant loop, oh, how we're entwined!

Shadows and Light

Shadows and light play tag in the park,
The sun takes a break, the moon leaves a mark.
We dance in the twilight, our feet take a flight,
Tripping on shadows, what a silly sight!

The cat's in the corner, plotting a scheme,
To chase down our laughter, it's more than a dream.
"I'm here!" says the shadow, "Just wait for a whim,
To pounce on your giggles—let's see who is slim!"

With flickers of joy, we twirl and we spin,
The world is a playground, let's jump right in!
The sun bursts with laughter, the night joins the fun,
In shadows and light, we become everyone.

So let's raise our voices, let silliness reign,
For in shadows and light, we can't be mundane.
Let's waltz with the dusk, and scamper with glee,
In this playful dance, just you and me!

Between Yesterday and Tomorrow

Where time takes a nap in a hammock so wide,
Yesterday laughs as tomorrow tries to hide.
We're stuck in a loop, in a whimsical race,
Chasing our futures with yesterday's face.

The clock's lost its hands, what a fool it can be,
Ticking and tocking, still late for tea.
We sip silly thoughts, slurp dreams down the line,
Mix knowing and guessing, it's all quite divine!

Yesterday whispers, "Remember this cheer?"
Tomorrow giggles, "Don't you dare disappear!"
In this merry dance, we move to the beat,
Between what we know and what's near to complete.

So let's play our game, in this timeless charade,
Where giggles collide and no moment's delayed.
In the realm of the silly, we'll laugh 'til we fall,
Between yesterday's pranks and tomorrow's mad call!

The Eternal Dance

In a whirl of feet, we spin with delight,
A dance of the ages, it's goofy tonight.
We leap with the stars, then trip on our toes,
With laughter and joy, the rhythm just flows.

The music is quirky, a tune of our weird,
And every misstep is met with a cheer.
The moon's our DJ, spinning tracks of the day,
As we twist and we turn, we just dance anyway!

Through giggles and grins, the world winks at us,
In this endless tango, come join the fuss.
Our hearts skip a beat, in perfect time's chase,
In the eternal dance, we find our own place.

So come take a twirl, let your spirit ignite,
In the fun of this dance, we shine oh so bright.
With every odd step, let's revel and prance,
For life is the tune, and we're lost in this dance!

The Ever-Knowing Heart

Roses are red, violets are blue,
My heart knows secrets, but won't tell you.
It beats in riddles, keeps them all tight,
Hiccups of laughter, day turns to night.

It whispers the truth in a wiggly way,
Like a fish on land, trying hard not to sway.
Jumping through hoops, it loves a good jest,
Silly as socks, but it thinks it's the best.

When you ask it questions, it giggles and twirls,
With answers wrapped in sparkles and swirls.
Oh, the wisdom of hearts, they dance and they prance,
In the carnival of life, it's a funny romance.

So come take a peek, embrace the bizarre,
The heart's got a joke, it's a real shining star.
Tickle the funny bone, let the chuckles start,
For humor and knowing are close, not apart.

Spirals of Understanding

Twists and turns, round we go,
Understanding's a dance, not a show.
Spirals of laughter in circles so tight,
Chasing the answers just out of sight.

A jiggle, a wiggle, the mind takes a spin,
What makes sense today, tomorrow's a grin.
Like spaghetti's journey from pot to the plate,
Understanding's tangled, but surely is great.

It giggles around in a playful embrace,
Finding new paths we can all trace.
Tickling thoughts like a bad tickle-fight,
We learn just enough to make it feel right.

Spinning and swirling like leaves in the breeze,
The more we react, the more we appease.
So let's take a ride on this merry-go-round,
In spirals of laughter, wisdom is found.

Beneath the Surface

Waves of the ocean, bubbles of jest,
Beneath the surface, it's all a big fest.
Octopuses juggling, fish in a hat,
A circus of secrets, how about that?

Dive deeper, they say, but watch for the splash,
Wisdom swims slow, like a shellfish bash.
With every tickle, the seaweed will grin,
Finding answers feels like a swim to win!

Where creatures conspire in undersea lore,
Sharing their dreams on the oceanic floor.
Knots of knowledge, tangled up tight,
It's a slippery dance, but we'll get it right.

Beneath the surface, hilarity bloats,
Like a whale in a tutu, while bobbing in boats.
Let's laugh with the dolphins, snicker with eels,
For all of these truths are the best-kept reels.

Enigmas of Existence

Who am I? A question so fun,
With answers that chirp like a confused bun.
Finding the why leaves us dizzy and spun,
Like a squirrel on caffeine, oh, what a run!

Existence is riddled with giggles and glee,
Unpacking the chaos, a sight to see.
Like umbrellas in storms, they flip and they flop,
Who knew life's mysteries liked to hop?

So we dance through the questions, a waltz and a jig,
Learning to laugh when the world feels too big.
For in every enigma, there's humor to find,
A punchline to life, so delightfully blind.

With jests from the universe, we strut and we fret,
Existing together, a funny duet.
Let's toast to the weird, to the quirky abyss,
In enigmas of life, there's always more bliss.

Memories Upon Memories

In a cupboard of socks, I find treasure,
Each pair tells a joke, brings me pleasure.
Last week's pizza slice, still in the box,
Whispers sweet tales, just like old flocks.

The cat wore a hat, twirling about,
Chasing its tail, with giggles and shout.
I tripped on the rug, made a fine mess,
Even the goldfish joined for the jest.

Grandpa recounts his wild youthful days,
Winking like wisdom, in funny ways.
Did he really wear spandex to the store?
Or was that just dream from the days of yore?

Maps of my mind, all folded and bent,
Show paths we took, with laughter and scent.
Each memory sprawls, a comic relief,
Turning my life into joy, not grief.

The Infinite Return

Round and round the sun goes spinning,
Like a dog chasing, never winning.
And just when you think you've found a break,
The cat steals the snack, just for the sake.

The clock strikes twelve, twice in a row,
Time playing tricks, a funny show.
I waved at my shadow, it waved back
We chuckled together, then I lost track.

Each tick-tock's a riddle, confusing the head,
As socks do hide under the bed.
I blink and it's morning, again and again,
With yesterday's cereal stuck to my chin.

Oh the stories we tell in a whirl of delight,
From the pancake disaster that happened last night.
The loop keeps us laughing, the joy that we earn,
For with every misstep, it's the infinite turn.

Time That Knows Itself

Time is a prankster, sly and spry,
Stealing my lunch, oh my, oh my!
It swipes my minutes, giggles in glee,
While I search for socks like a lost bumblebee.

Calendar pages do a little dance,
Each day a circus, if given a chance.
Yesterday's antics, they haunt me so,
As I dive into Friday, only to slow.

With whispers of futures, and echoes of past,
Time says, 'Don't worry, the fun's going fast!'
But I'm stuck in a loop, even my clock sighs,
It's hard to keep up with such crafty lies.

Yet in every tick and the sly moments heard,
Life sings a jingle, so sweetly absurd.
With each passing second, we uncover the jest,
In this playful enigma, we find the best.

The Resounding Cycle of Insight

Round and round we spin like a whirlpool,
Insights echo like laughter; aren't we the fools?
I ponder my thoughts while making a pie,
All the ingredients laughing—oh my, oh my!

With wisdom like rubber, it bounces around,
In the kitchen, my brain makes a silly sound.
The carrots conspire with the cabbage to scheme,
Creating a salad, a rascally dream.

In circles we gather, each thought shared anew,
With every retelling, the jokes seem to woo.
Playful reflections that perfect our day,
Turning the mundane into a grand ballet.

So let the cycle spin, with giggles and cheers,
With echoes of thoughts that span all our years.
For wisdom is funny, a joy to inspect,
In this wobbly dance, we find our respect.

Ties that Bind

In a world where time unwinds,
Socks still lost in daily finds.
Two left shoes upon the floor,
Strangely tied, yet we want more.

Odd quirks that we've come to know,
Like a plant that won't dare grow.
Fuzzy logic with a twist,
Amusing chaos, can't resist!

Friends who text and miss the point,
Jokes that shine but often disappoint.
Yet through laughter, bonds are formed,
In strange ties, we are warmed.

Round and round, it's quite the game,
Futility has its own name.
With humor, life's fabric's spun,
Together we laugh, we all have fun.

Mirrors of the Soul

Reflections dance in silly ways,
Mirror faces stuck in praise.
Bouncing back our jester's grin,
Flip the world, let the fun begin!

Giggling goblins all around,
Silly shadows that astound.
What they see, we're yet to know,
In the funhouse, we steal the show.

Twisted truths that we can share,
With each twist, we shed despair.
Finding wisdom in the jest,
In mirrored laughs, we feel the best.

Echoes mix, and time will pause,
In this madness, we find cause.
Through winks and grins, we'll cue the tune,
In every laugh, our hearts attune.

Wisdom's Fabric

Threads of folly, stitched with care,
Fabric woven, oh so rare.
In every crease, a funny tale,
Life's plaid patterns never pale.

Quirky seams and mismatched dyes,
Hiding truth in playful lies.
With each knot, we knot our fate,
Rumbling laughter that feels so great.

Wisdom's garment feels so light,
Worn by jesters in the night.
A patchwork of the wise and bold,
Their funny tales are warmly told.

Stitch by stitch, we weave our dreams,
Tangled paths and daylight beams.
In this fabric, joy will twine,
In silly moments, we'll define.

The Recurring Theme

Round and round, we tell the tale,
Of curious cats that cannot fail.
Each cycle brings new laughter's chime,
In every step, a dance with time.

The rooster crows, the dog debates,
Life's strange puzzles; all our fates.
With each circle, the fun expands,
Looping joy with twisted hands.

Chasing tails and spinning news,
Arguments over ancient views.
Yet through the quirks, we find our way,
In recurring laughs that save the day.

With each revisit, jests will thrive,
In this dance, we feel alive.
Embracing silliness, we'll glean,
Forever caught in this routine.

The Echo Chamber of Existence

In a room full of echoes, we laugh and we shout,
The questions we ponder, they twist all about.
What goes in must come out, or so it is said,
Yet the jokes we retell are stuck in our head.

A parrot named Polly is speaking my mind,
Repeating my thoughts, it's one of a kind.
The walls seem to giggle, the ceiling a clown,
As my sanity slowly starts tumbling down.

Reflections of nonsense bounce off every wall,
As I trip on the carpet, I start to enthrall.
With a grin, I declare, I'm a genius today,
In this chamber of echoes, I'll surely be gay.

So here in the oddness, I find my delight,
With laughter that echoes well into the night.
Embracing the absurdity, I find my own bliss,
In a room full of echoes that I can't dismiss.

A Journey Through Self and Time

I packed up my past in a suitcase of dreams,
With socks from the future, or so it seems.
On a train made of wishes, I took a seat,
But the ride to my destiny has fanciful feet.

The conductor, a turtle, said, "Where to, my friend?"
"To find where it started, or just where it ends?"
I chuckled and answered, "Let's go for a spin!"
Then we both snoozed off, let the odd game begin.

We passed by my childhood, full of bright bouncing balls,

A year made of candy, with peppermint halls.
But when I woke up, what a sight on the rail,
The turtle was laughing; I'd totally failed.

Now I roam through the cosmos with giggles in tow,
Exploring the quirks of this life's sweet tableau.
Though the journey is wacky, I'll wave as I climb,
For all that I seek is both silly and sublime.

The Spiral of Awareness

Like a dog chasing tails, I spin round and round,
Each thought a lost nugget, but oh, they abound.
I try to be aware, but the circles won't cease,
In a spiral of giggles, I find my sweet peace.

My inner self whispers, "Just go with the flow,"
But each twist brings a giggle, a shimmer, a glow.
I tumble through clarity, a dizzying dance,
Where sense loses meaning; it's a comical chance!

The answers keep flipping, like a pancake in air,
With syrupy wisdom that's sticky and rare.
I laugh as I spiral, the questions in spree,
In this merry-go-round of confounding glee.

With each spin of insight, a chuckle I find,
In the whirl of existence, the laughter, it's kind.
So onward I spiral, in joyfully jest,
For the dance is delightful, a mental fest!

Infinite Knowings

In the library of quirks, I browse through the shelves,
Where knowledge is wobbly, like marshmallows' selves.
With books that are giggling, they talk as you read,
Infinite knowings, but none that you need.

The librarian chuckles; he's juggling my thoughts,
With a wink, he confides, "They're all tangled like knots!"

But I roam through the pages of paradox fun,
Finding wisdom's reflections tangled under the sun.

What do I know in this circus of minds?
That my jokes have a punchline that no one here finds.
As I flip through the stories of things I cannot see,
I chuckle at knowings that giggle at me.

Each answer a riddle that leads to more jest,
In this infinite comedy, I feel so blessed.
So I dance through the volumes, a whimsical chase,
In the land of the funny, I've found my own place.

Timeless Echoes

Time is a rubber band, stretching high into space,
With echoes of laughter that never leave a trace.
I bounce off the moments, like a rubbery child,
With timeless adventures so silly and wild.

I met a wise owl who wore funny pink shoes,
He said time was a joke, "You can't ever lose!"
With a tick and a tock, we danced 'round the clock,
In this timeless old playground, we'd twist, laugh, and rock.

Every second's a giggle, every minute a smile,
As I skip through the hourglass, adding more style.
The past hums a tune, the future plays catch,
And I'm here in the echo, the perfect mismatched.

In laughter, I linger, a wraith of delight,
In the cozy embrace of a whimsical night.
Timeless echoes keep calling, with jokes to employ,
In the garden of nonsense, I flourish with joy.

Wisdom's Dual Path

Two roads diverge in a funny way,
One leads to night, the other to day.
I took the wrong path, or so they say,
Or maybe it's right, just in disarray.

The signs are cheesy, with silly puns,
While squirrels debate who has more buns.
A wise old owl says, "Don't fear the runs!"
Knowledge is wacky, and oh, it just funs!

A map in circles, a guide that's bent,
Lessons in laughter, no need to repent.
Step on a toe, it's all accidental,
Finding the truth can be quite experimental.

So let's juggle thoughts, let ideas collide,
Embrace the chaos, let nonsense be tried.
In wisdom's circus, we'll laugh, not hide,
Two paths to travel, let humor be our guide.

Unraveling the Endless Thread

In a tapestry bright, yarns intertwine,
A cat named Whiskers, she likes to dine.
Tug at the string, it leads to a shrine,
Where giggles and snickers, are truly divine.

The weaver is dizzy, lost in her art,
Knots getting tangled, oh where do we start?
Each loop is a riddle, a sneeze or a fart,
A knot in the thread brings a laugh to the heart.

Questions like yarn balls, they spin here and there,
Each twist a puzzle, let's have a scare!
Laughter unravels, a joy beyond compare,
The endless thread of knowing, silly as air.

So let's roll the spool, give it a whirl,
Unravel and giggle, let knowledge unfurl.
In laughter, we find what insanity's swirl,
For each batty thread, brings fun to the world.

The Loop of Understanding

Round and round in a dizzying flight,
Chasing truth like a dog chasing light.
With each little bark, I might get it right,
But where's the end point? Oh what a sight!

The questions keep spinning, a canine's delight,
"Is a bone just a stick? Oh give me a fright!"
With each wagging tail, a clue takes flight,
Understanding in loops, oh what a bite!

When fetching the ball, I think and I ponder,
Is the chase just a game or a laugh to wander?
As I spin in circles, my thoughts start to squander,
Sniffing for wisdom, my mind grows fonder.

So let's chase our tails, with curiosity fine,
In circles of jest, let's sip on some wine.
In the loop of our thinking, joy's the best sign,
For understanding is funny, like intertwining twine.

When Questions Become Their Answers

What's the sound of one hand clapping? Ha!
An echo of wisdom, a cosmic guffaw.
A question like gum, it sticks with a flaw,
Yet answers float 'round like an old grandma's shawl.

Why does the chicken cross? It's quite absurd,
To get to the other side, oh haven't you heard?
The answers are chuckles, both silly and blurred,
In a world of old jokes, where punchlines are stirred.

Each riddle, a ruckus, a tumbler of shakes,
Why not ask Neptune why he keeps his lakes?
When questions become giggles, life truly takes,
A twist of humor that giggling makes.

So poke at these queries, dance with each laugh,
For the answers we seek are a funny little half.
In the realm of confusion, let's share the path,
When questions meet humor, oh what a gaffe!

Journeys Without End

Tripping over thoughts and dreams,
Ice cream cones and glittered streams,
We chase our tails in curious plays,
While time just giggles, lost in a haze.

A map drawn upside down and backwards,
We dance with socks, in our own awkward,
Every road leads to a town of jest,
Where logic laughs and spouts its best.

Bicycles roll on rooftops high,
As turtles sprint, we wonder why,
Our compass spins like a dizzy bird,
While Spaghetti trees offer words absurd.

In endless loops we find our bliss,
Oh, what a world with a tartar sauce kiss,
The journey is wacky, a glorious bend,
Forever starting, never an end.

The Vast Terrain of Mind

Deep jungles of memory, wild and free,
Where monkeys ponder philosophy,
Clouds of laughter drift over the sea,
As thoughts explode like popcorn, whee!

Mountains of nonsense scrape the sky,
With valleys where giggles never die,
Exploring spaces where sentences roam,
Chasing wild rhymes as we wander home.

Caves filled with riddles and quests unknown,
Mushrooms whisper, 'This mind's our throne,'
Echoes of nonsense push back the light,
In this vast terrain, chaos feels right.

So let's map the terrain with playful glee,
Through neurons that dance, wait and see,
A mental expedition, comedy's jam,
Isn't this brain a fun little scam?

Cycles of Perception

Spin me round in circles vast,
Round and round, the die is cast,
What was once clear turns opaque,
Dance with the shivers, make no mistake.

I saw a cat that wore a tie,
Dancing whilst questioning why,
Each look a joke, a twist of fate,
Are we the punchline? Can't contemplate.

Mirrors bounce, reflecting truths,
Typewriters tap while sipping smooth,
Shells of laughter stuck in our ears,
As wisdom slips like fallen tears.

In cycles we find the zany peace,
Confusion's song will never cease,
So let's join hands in this whirling game,
In laughter's cycle, we're all the same.

The Infinite Within

An onion deep, layers unwind,
In each one, a new thought aligned,
Dancing with wisdom, round we go,
As secrets hide in a windswept blow.

The clock laughs and loses its time,
Counting giggles in perfect mime,
We dig for truth in the cookie jar,
Finding crumbs that lead us far.

Exploring the depths with spoons and spades,
Inventing tomorrows through yesterday's charades,
In this cosmic joke, we find our line,
The infinite whispers, 'You're still divine.'

Enjoy the ride inside your head,
Where absurdity flourishes, joy is bred,
In the garden of knowing, tickled and thin,
There lies the adventure, the infinite within.